Also by Bob Hartman:
The Precious Pearl
The Busy Builders
One Sheep Short
Bob Hartman's Rhyming Bible
The Link-it-Up Bible
The Tell-it-Together Gospel

The Lion Storyteller Bible 25th Anniversary Edition
Welcome to the Journey
Where Do I Come from?

————

The original version of this story is found in the Gospel of Luke, where Jesus tells a parable:

'If a man has a hundred sheep and one of them gets lost, what will he do? Won't he leave the ninety-nine others in the wilderness and go to search for the one that is lost until he finds it? And when he has found it, he will joyfully carry it home on his shoulders. When he arrives, he will call together his friends and neighbors, saying, 'Rejoice with me because I have found my lost sheep.' In the same way, there is more joy in heaven over one lost sinner who repents and returns to God than over ninety-nine others who are righteous and haven't strayed away!
Luke 15: 1–7 (New Living Translation)

————

First published in Great Britain in 2022

Society for Promoting Christian Knowledge
36 Causton Street, London SW1P 4ST
www.spck.org.uk

British Library Cataloguing-in-Publication Data
A catalogue record for this book is avaliable from the British Library

ISBN 978–0–281–08539–2

Printed by Imago

Produced on paper from sustainable forests

Bob Hartman

ONE SHEEP SHORT

Fantastic illustrations by

Mark Beech

spck

The Pharisees,
the Pharisees,
the Pharisees were fine.

But then they
looked at Jesus,
and those with
whom he dined.

4

The Pharisees,
the Pharisees,
the Pharisees were fine.
'Why do you eat with sinners?'
they all complained and whined.

So Jesus told a story,
of a sheep that went away,
and how the shepherd went to find
his lost and lonely stray.

They shut the door, flopped on the floor,
quite happy to recline.

But out among the wolves and bears,
one sheep had gone astray.

She'd tried to find the path back home,
but, sadly, lost her way.

They had a brew, then made a stew
of fresh-picked dandelions.

But when the shepherd came to count,
his face turned sad and grey.
'I do believe I'm one sheep short,'
he whispered in dismay.

The ninety-nine,
the ninety-nine,
the ninety-nine were fine.
'But we're still here,' they bleated clear.
'Do have a glass of wine!'

'I'm glad you're fine,'
the shepherd said.
'I simply cannot stay.

16

I'll leave you ninety-nine behind
and find my one lost stray.'

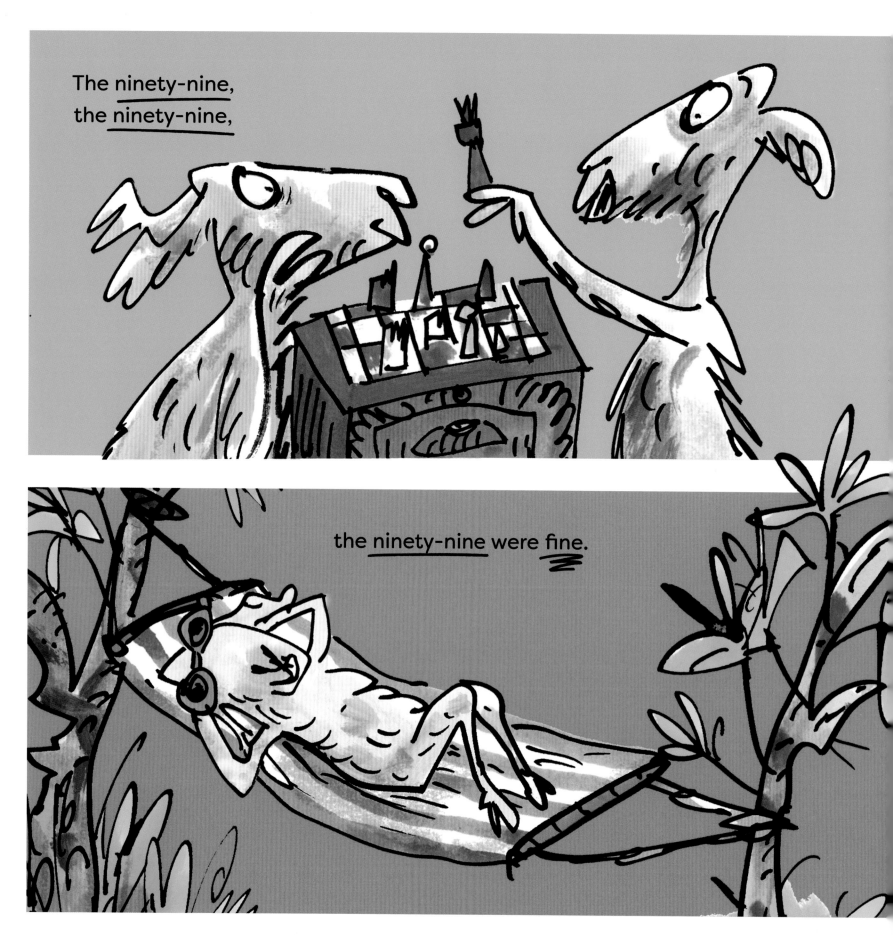

'Such a fuss!' they huffed and puffed.

'Where does he find the time?'

19

The shepherd went into the wild,

as night eclipsed the day.

'My sheep is lost,

I'll pay whatever price I have to pay!'

The ninety-nine, the ninety-nine, the ninety-nine were fine.

They made their beds, laid down their heads and read some nursery rhymes.

Torn by thorns and bruised by rocks,
the shepherd made his way.

His sacrifice rewarded,
when, at last, he found his stray!

25

They snuggled there,
without a care
for the sheep they'd left behind.

The shepherd brought his sheep back home

and, shouting his hoorays,

Welcome home!

he partied with his neighbours

till night turned
into day!

29

'But I'm just like that shepherd,'
is all he had to say.
'To find the lost, I'll pay whatever
price I have to pay.'